D1307234

IndyCar
RACING

By P. K. Daniel

SportsZone
An Imprint of Abdo Publishing
www.abdopublishing.com

www.abdopublishing.com

Published by Abdo Publishing, a division of ABDO, PO Box 398166, Minneapolis, Minnesota 55439. Copyright © 2015 by Abdo Consulting Group, Inc. International copyrights reserved in all countries. No part of this book may be reproduced in any form without written permission from the publisher. SportsZone™ is a trademark and logo of Abdo Publishing.

Printed in the United States of America, North Mankato, Minnesota
032014
092014

Cover Photo: Alex Gallardo/AP Images
Interior Photos: Alex Gallardo/AP Images, 1; AJ Mast/AP Images, 4–5; Michael Conroy/AP Images, 6; Paul Sancya/AP Images, 8; Seth Rossman/AP Images, 10; Henry Ford/AP Images, 12–13; Darron Cummings/AP Images, 14; Kemp Smith/AP Images, 17; AP Images, 19; Hodag Media/Shutterstock Images, 20–21; Brian Patterson Photos/Shutterstock Images, 22; Cal Sport Media/AP Images, 24; Photo Works/Shutterstock Images, 26–27, 36–37; PhotoStock10/Shutterstock Images, 28–29; Shutterstock Images, 30; Tom Pennington/AP Images, 32; LAT, Michael L. Levitt/AP Images, 34; Carlos Orsorio/AP Images, 39; Mary Altaffer/AP Images, 40; Michael G McKinne/Shutterstock Images, 43; Mike Carlson/AP Images, 45

Editor: Patrick Donnelly
Series Designer: Craig Hinton

Library of Congress Control Number: 2014932866

Cataloging-in-Publication Data
Daniel, P.K.
 IndyCar racing / P.K. Daniel.
  p. cm. -- (Inside the speedway)
Includes bibliographical references and index.
ISBN 978-1-62403-404-6
1. Automobile racing--Juvenile literature. 2. Indianapolis Speedway Race--Juvenile literature. I. Title.
796.72--dc23

2014932866

TABLE OF CONTENTS

chapter 1

THE RACE THAT GOT AWAY

n 2011, a rookie driver almost pulled off an amazing upset. It was the 100th anniversary of the Indianapolis 500, also known as the Indy 500. J. R. Hildebrand had only a few hundred yards to go. He was about to win "The Greatest Spectacle in Racing." But disaster struck on the last turn of the last lap.

Hildebrand went to pass a lapped car. Instead, he crashed into the wall. His dream of winning the race ended. Dan Wheldon

Dan Wheldon speeds past J. R. Hildebrand to win the 2011 Indianapolis 500.

Brazilian Tony Kanaan poses with the winner's trophy after his victory in the 2013 Indianapolis 500.

swooped by Hildebrand to win his second Indy 500 title. Wheldon took home $2.5 million in winnings.

Exciting moments like that are common in IndyCar racing. The IndyCar Series is the top open-wheel racing series in the United States. Open wheel means the tires are outside the car's main body. The cars are different from those you see on the street in many other ways, too. Their tires do not have fenders like regular cars. Drivers sit in the only seat in an open cockpit. The cars are powered by engines that produce rocket-like thrust. Many of these features allow IndyCars to go much faster than stock cars. However, they are also difficult to control.

The Indianapolis 500 is IndyCar's most famous race. It takes place over Memorial Day weekend each May. The race is the elite event of the IndyCar Series. It is raced over 500 miles (805 km). Indianapolis Motor Speedway is one of the world's most famous tracks. More than 250,000 fans watch from the stands and thousands more from the infield at its 2.5-mile (4 km) oval course for the Indy 500.

The IndyCar Series is all about speed. It is the fastest series in the world. Cars reach speeds of up to 230 miles per hour (370 km/h).

Feeding the Fans

Each year more than 250,000 fans attend the Indy 500, and boy are they hungry! Combined, they go through:

- more than 10,000 pounds (4,535 kg) of hamburgers. That is equal to the weight of six IndyCars.
- more than 24,000 pounds (10,886 kg) of fries. That is the same as the weight of two adult elephants.
- more than 475 gallons (1,798 liters) of ketchup. That is enough to fill up 10 bathtubs.

They wash it all down with more than 16,000 gallons (60,567 L) of soda. That would fill two tanker trucks.

Gil de Ferran holds the world speed record for the fastest lap. He averaged 241.428 mph (388.541 km/h) at the California Speedway in 2000. De Ferran won the Indianapolis 500 in 2003.

All of that speed brings additional risks, though. The IndyCar Series is considered the most difficult racing series in the world. It is also the most dangerous. High speeds often lead to accidents. At such high speeds, those accidents can be fatal. Wheldon died in a 15-car crash at the IndyCar World Championships just five months after his win over Hildebrand.

Many IndyCar drivers come from the United States. Several come from other countries. They race on different kinds of tracks. Many races are held on oval-shaped tracks. But some are held on permanent road courses and street courses. Indianapolis Motor Speedway is an example of a permanent track. The Grand Prix of Long Beach is held on a temporary

Dan Wheldon was a fan favorite who died in a crash in 2011.

street course. In that race, turbocharged cars rumble through

closed-off city streets.

A point system determines the IndyCar Series champion.

Drivers are awarded points based on where they finish in each race. Also, a driver who leads at least one lap receives one bonus point. The driver who leads the most laps receives two bonus points. The driver with the most points at the end of the season wins the title and more than $1 million in prize money.

Remembering a Champion

Former racing rivals gathered in October 2013 to celebrate the life and honor the legacy of Dan Wheldon. The two-time Indianapolis 500 winner died in a crash at Las Vegas Motor Speedway in 2011. Scott Dixon was among those at the inaugural Dan Wheldon Memorial Pro-Am Karting Challenge. The drivers participated in a pro-am race.

chapter 2

HISTORY AT THE BRICKYARD

The IndyCar Series name is directly linked to the famous race, the Indianapolis 500. The race has been around for a long time. The first race took place in 1911. The Championship Auto Racing Team (CART), which later became the Champ Car World Series, has governed open-wheel racing in the United States since 1979. The Indy Racing League (IRL) formed and began racing in 1996. This choice for drivers led to a split

Racers line up at the start of the first Indianapolis 500 in 1911.

that continued for a dozen years. IRL and Champ Car reunited in 2008 under the IRL umbrella. But open-wheel racing was again known as the IndyCar Series. In 2011, the IRL name was officially dropped in favor of IndyCar.

The IRL oversees the IndyCar Series. It also controls the developmental or minor league series. The developmental series includes Indy Lights, the Pro Mazda Championship, and the Cooper Tires USF2000 National Championship.

The Indy 500 is rich in history and pageantry. One tradition is singing "Back Home Again in Indiana" before the start of the race. Hundreds of multicolored balloons are released when the last note is sung.

One of the most recognizable traditions happens shortly after the race. The winning drivers are handed a bottle of cold milk. They gulp the milk, usually dribbling it down their chins. That tradition started in 1933. Louis Meyer asked for a glass of buttermilk after winning the race. He won the Indy 500 again in 1936. This time, he received a bottle of buttermilk instead of a glass.

Brickyard Basics

Indianapolis Motor Speedway is the world's largest spectator sporting facility. It has more than 250,000 permanent seats. They would measure nearly 100 miles (161 km) if laid end to end. It is also known as the Brickyard. The original surface was crushed rock and tar. Shortly after, in 1909, it was replaced with 3.2 million street-paving bricks. Eventually, rough spots had to be paved over. Today, only a three-foot (0.9 m) strip of bricks remains. After the race, the winning drivers and their crews kiss those bricks to celebrate. NASCAR driver Dale Jarrett started the tradition after he won the Brickyard 400 in 1996. Indy 500 drivers also honor that tradition.

A local dairy decided to get in on the action. The next year, the dairy gave the winner a bottle of milk. By 1956, the tradition had stuck. But today, winners have a choice. They can request skim, 2 percent, or whole milk.

The winner also wears a ring of 33 flowers. The wreath also features 33 miniature checkered flags mixed with red, white, and blue ribbons.

The champion also receives the historic Borg-Warner Trophy. Inscribed on the trophy is the

Dan Wheldon kisses the yard of bricks remaining at the Indianapolis Motor Speedway after winning the 2005 Indy 500.

driver's name, the date, and the average speed during the race. It also has a small likeness of the winner's face on it. The trophy is made of sterling silver and stands more than five feet (1.52 meters) tall. It weighs nearly 153 pounds (69.3 kg). The winners do not get to take the huge trophy home. They get a miniature version of the trophy.

Most IndyCar drivers are men. But many women have participated in the Indianapolis 500. Janet Guthrie was the first of nine women to race there. She raced in it from 1977 to 1979. Guthrie was followed by Lyn St. James, Sarah Fisher, Danica Patrick, Milka Duno, Simona de Silvestro, Ana Beatriz Figuereido, Pippa Mann, and Katherine Legge.

Ray Harroun won the first Indianapolis 500 in 1911. He was nicknamed "The Little Professor" because he designed cars. Harroun helped design and build the car he drove in the Indy 500. The single-seat car was painted yellow and black. It was called the Marmon Wasp. The Wasp has since been restored. It is on permanent display at the Indianapolis Motor Speedway Hall of Fame Museum.

Before Harroun, Indy cars had two seats. One was for the driver. The other held a riding mechanic. The riding mechanic would watch for the other cars. He would also repair the car during the race.

Ray Harroun drives the Marmon Wasp to victory at the first Indy 500 in 1911.

Harroun did not use a riding mechanic. He could see the cars behind him. He had taken a piece of mirror and framed it in steel. He attached it to the dashboard. Today all cars use one of these. They are called rearview mirrors.

The rearview mirror is just one invention that came from IndyCar racing. Race technology has led to many new or improved features in the cars we drive. Those features include tires, disc brakes, and safety harnesses, like those used in child safety seats.

chapter 3

BUILT FOR RACING

ndyCar vehicles are open-wheel, single-seat cars. They differ from cars you would see on the streets. Those cars have fenders that cover the wheels. Open-wheel cars are typically built for racing. They are usually technically superior to other styles of race cars. The engine is usually located behind the driver. The rear wheels move the car. Those wheels do the pushing while the front wheels do

IndyCar vehicles are built for speed.

Honda is one of the two manufacturers that supply engines for all cars in the IndyCar Series.

the steering. Open-wheel cars also have open cockpits. That means the driver's head is exposed.

These sleek cars are built to be aerodynamic. That means they can move through the air with less wind resistance. A more aerodynamic car can move faster while using less fuel. The front and rear wing on the car work together to keep it balanced. The wings are adjustable to improve handling. Balance is a key to winning.

Honda and Chevrolet supply the engines for all of the cars in the IndyCar Series. Honda had been the only supplier for a time. Chevrolet returned in 2012. That brought back competition between the engine manufacturers. The Manufacturers Award goes to the engine manufacturer that scores the most points in a season. Chevrolet won the Manufacturers Award with a dual turbocharger in 2013. Honda went with a single turbocharger. Starting in 2014, all engines have to include dual turbochargers. Turbochargers increase an engine's power by squeezing more air into the cylinder. That allows more fuel to be added.

IndyCars use Firestone Firehawk racing radials for

The Fan Experience

IndyCar drivers zip around the track on race day. Now fans can be "backseat" drivers with IndyCar 13. The mobile app provides a collage of live race videos. Cameras in the cars provide streaming video of select racers. Fans can listen to drivers talking with their pit crews. They also can see live race results and updated standings.

Firestone Firehawk radials are the official tire of IndyCar drivers.

the tires. The tire sidewalls have to be strong enough to handle the high speeds of a race car. They also have to be thin enough to handle the heat generated by the high speeds. The front tires are about 11 inches (28 cm) wide. The rear tires are just a bit wider at 15 inches (38 cm).

IndyCar vehicles run on 100 percent fuel-grade ethanol. It works well in high-performance cars. The cars do not lose any horsepower or speed using ethanol. In previous seasons, the cars used methanol, another fuel alternative. Today's cars burn much less fuel by using ethanol.

The cars can produce between 550 and 700 horsepower and can reach nearly 230 mph (370 km/h). The speed and power of IndyCars can make races exciting.

1. **FRONT WING:** Works with the rear wing to create aerodynamic downforce. It can be adjusted for different tracks and during a race to improve handling.

2. **REAR WING:** Like the front wing, it can be adjusted for superspeedway, intermediate tracks, and short ovals/road courses.

3. **CHASSIS:** Includes the frame, wheels, engine, and driver's compartment. It is made of carbon fiber with an aluminum honeycomb core.

4. **FRONT/REAR SUSPENSION:** Keeps the ride feeling smooth and helps the driver maintain control during braking and accelerating.

5. **FRONTAL HEAD RESTRAINT:** This safety item is required for all IndyCar drivers. It reduces the likelihood of head and neck injuries in a crash.

6. **TIRES:** Tire tread heats up and becomes tar-like during high-speed racing, helping the tires grip the track.

chapter 4

DRIVER'S ED

Being an IndyCar driver requires commitment and a lot of training. There are three primary ways to enter the sport. Drivers can train through karting, the Soap Box Derby, and the Mazda Road to Indy.

Karting is one of the most popular paths. Many IndyCar Series stars began their careers by racing go-karts. A go-kart is a small, motorized car with an open top. It is used especially for racing.

Many IndyCar drivers get their start by racing go-karts.

Four organizations host national events throughout the season. They are the World Karting Association, International Karting Federation, SuperKarts! USA, and Rotax.

The Soap Box Derby is for nonmotorized cars. Soap box races start at a ramp on top of a hill. The cars rely on gravity for power. They can reach speeds of 35 mph (51 km/h).

This type of racing attracts more than 5,000 competitors worldwide each year. They compete in various regional organizations and events. Racers compete in three divisions. Boys and girls ages seven through 13 compete in the Stock division. They build simple cars from purchased kits. The Super Stock Car division is for boys and girls ages nine through 18. They build larger, heavier models, also from kits. The Masters division is for boys and girls ages 10 through 18. They also use purchased kits, but they can use creativity and design skills to make more sophisticated cars.

The season concludes at the All-American Soap Box Derby Nationals in Akron, Ohio. The race has been held each July since 1934. Racers compete for scholarship awards and prizes.

Drivers who are more serious about racing enter the Mazda Road to Indy. It is the minor league for drivers who want to compete in the IndyCar Series. It features the Skip Barber Racing School. The school awards scholarships totaling over $2 million. Drivers race IndyCars in three different series.

They train on oval courses, permanent road courses, and street circuits. The best drivers advance to the IndyCar Series. The training also helps to prepare engineers and mechanics for the IndyCar Series.

Driving schools teach participants how to handle a high-powered speed machine. Drivers practice many skills needed to succeed as racers. Racing an IndyCar requires much more skill than meets the eye. Drivers must master basic skills such as starting and restarting. Braking and passing are also essential skills. As drivers progress, they learn more advanced skills such as drafting, cornering, and downshifting. Drafting is using the stream of air from the car directly in front to go faster and

Colorful Communication

Colored flags are used to communicate with drivers during races. A green flag represents the start of the race. A yellow flag means caution. A red and yellow striped flag means there is a hazard on the track. It could be debris or a spot made slippery by oil or another substance. A white flag flies when the leader starts his final lap. A checkered flag signifies the end of the race.

IndyCars often race directly behind another car to conserve energy. This is called drafting.

conserve energy. Cornering is how a driver approaches a turn. Downshifting is putting the car into a lower gear to give it more power.

Physical fitness is also part of driver training. Drivers must be in top physical condition to be able to drive up to four hours at high speeds. Drivers do endurance training, weight training, and reaction training. They do cardio workouts to increase their endurance. That is because they only get to rest during eight-second pit stops. Weight training helps to strengthen the neck, shoulders, and core. That helps drivers endure the g-forces produced in racing. G-force, or gravity force, is the weight felt on your body when speed increases.

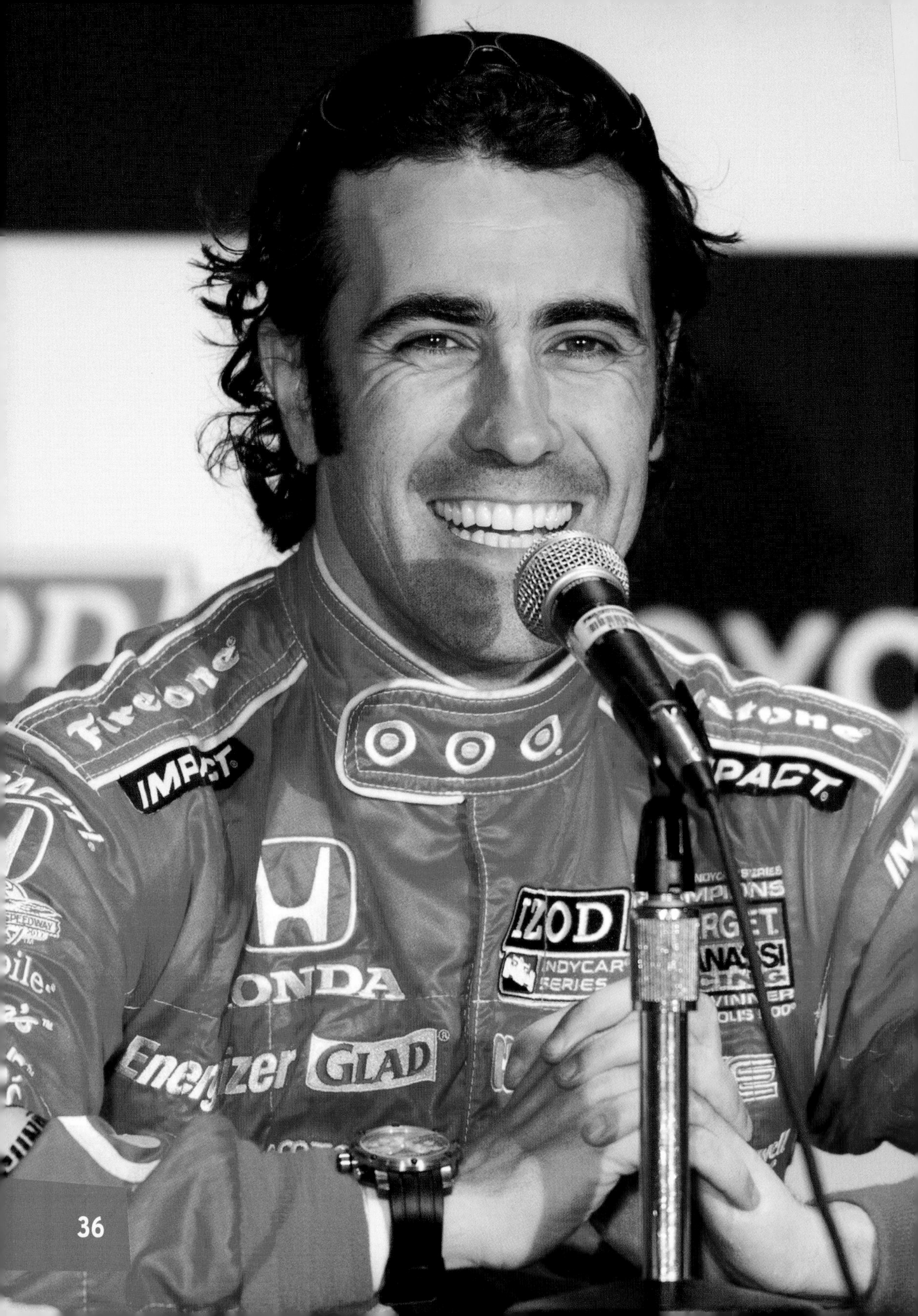
IMPACT
HONDA
Energizer
GLAD
IZOD
INDYCAR
SERIES

chapter 5

TRACK STARS

ndyCar racing has produced several stars known around the world. Three drivers have won the Indianapolis 500 four times each through 2013. A. J. Foyt won three times in the 1960s and again in 1977. Al Unser won three titles in the 1970s and one more in 1987. Rick Mears won four times between 1979 and 1991. Unser was the oldest ever to win the Indy 500. He was 47 years, 360 days old when he won his final Indy 500.

Dario Franchitti won the Indy 500 three times and was a four-time IndyCar Series champion.

Drivers earn prize money for how they finish in the Indianapolis 500. The total purse has gone up over the years. Emerson Fittipaldi was the first driver to earn $1 million in one year. He won the 1989 race. The winner's share for Fittipaldi and his team that year was $1,001,604. Today's winners bring home more than twice that much.

Brazilian Helio Castroneves raced the Indy 500 for the first two times in 2001 and 2002. He won both tries. Nobody had ever done that before. Only five drivers have won two straight Indy 500s. Castroneves was the first to do it since Unser in 1970 and 1971. He was also the youngest. He was only 27 years old when he won his second Indy 500. He added a third Indy 500 title in 2009.

Castroneves had a tradition that made him even more famous. He climbed the fence around the track after each win. The likeable driver also found success on the dance floor and on TV. He was a champion on ABC's *Dancing with the Stars*.

He was also a correspondent for *Entertainment Tonight*.

Scottish driver Dario Franchitti won his third Indianapolis 500 in 2012. He was a four-time IndyCar Series champion (2007, 2009, 2010, and 2011). He also was married to actress Ashley Judd. He had hoped to race longer. However, Franchitti was seriously injured in a crash in 2013. That forced him to retire at age 40. He ended his career tied for eighth all-time with 31 IndyCar victories. He was the oldest IndyCar Series champion in 2011 at age 38 years, 4 months, and 27 days. Sam

Women Make History

IndyCar racing has a long history of including female drivers. And several women have held their own in the sport. Danica Patrick is the most successful female driver in the history of US open-wheel racing. She is the only woman to win an IndyCar Series race. She won the Indy Japan 300 in 2008. She placed third in the 2009 Indianapolis 500. That was the highest finish ever by a woman. Sarah Fisher is the first and only female team owner. Through 2013 she also had the most starts (nine) for a woman in the history of the Indy 500.

Simona de Silvestro is making a name for herself. She was the only female driver who competed full-time in 2013. IndyCar team owner Jimmy Vasser has called her the "best female racer on the planet." De Silvestro joined Fisher and Patrick as the only female drivers to finish in the top three in an IndyCar race. She finished second to Scott Dixon at the Grand Prix of Houston in 2013.

Hornish Jr. was the youngest at 22 years, 3 months, 4 days in 2001.

The Andretti family left its mark on IndyCar racing. Mario Andretti was a four-time IndyCar champion. He also won the 1969 Indy 500 and was the 1978 Formula One world champion. His son Michael won 42 races as a driver and another 48 as an owner. Michael's son Marco finished second in his first Indianapolis 500 in 2006. Mario Andretti was a character voice in the 2013 movie *Turbo*. The movie is about an ordinary garden snail who dreams of winning the Indianapolis 500.

Through 2013, Scott Dixon has one Indianapolis 500 title and three IndyCar championships (2003, 2008, and 2013). Both of his parents were dirt-track racers in their native New Zealand. Dixon drove his first race car at age 13. To see over the steering wheel, he sat on a cushion attached to his pants. In fact, his most embarrassing moment came when he crashed

Scott Dixon is a three-time IndyCar series champion whose parents were both dirt-track racers in his native New Zealand.

as a young driver. When he got out of the car, everyone could

see the cushion tied to his backside.

Graham Rahal is the son of 1986 Indianapolis 500 winner Bobby Rahal. Graham became the youngest race winner in IndyCar history when he was 19. He won the Honda Grand Prix of St. Petersburg in 2008 in his first IndyCar Series race. He connects with his fans through social media tools like Twitter, Facebook, and Instagram. He also launched his own app to share even more about his life with his fans.

However, the best way for drivers to connect with their fans is at the track. From the early days of the Indianapolis 500 to the modern era of the IndyCar Series, fans have been drawn to the thrills and danger of this exciting form of racing. Technology and safety continue to improve conditions and intensify competition from the pole position to the checkered flag. Drivers have become household names throughout the world. And the future looks bright for IndyCar racing for years to come.

GLOSSARY

CAUTION PERIOD
A time when drivers must slow down because the track has become unsafe due to an accident, debris, or bad weather.

CHECKERED FLAG
A flag of black and white squares waved when the winner crosses the finish line.

DOWNFORCE
The combination of resistance and gravity that keeps cars on the ground. This downward thrust is created by aerodynamics. It is especially important in turns.

DRAFTING
The practice of following closely behind another car to take advantage of the air pressure created by the lead car. A driver can either use the draft to pass cars or to lift off the gas pedal slightly to conserve fuel.

FENDER
A piece of metal or plastic that protects the wheel from splashing mud and water or other debris.

INFIELD
The area inside the boundary of the track.

OPEN WHEEL
Refers to any type of race car that does not have wheels enclosed within fenders.

PIT
The area where cars come in for fuel, tires, adjustments, and repairs during on-track sessions.

POLE POSITION
The first car in line at the start of a race.

FOR MORE *INFORMATION*

Further Readings

Arute, Jack. *Jack Arute's Tales from the Indianapolis 500*. Champaign, IL: Sports Publishing LLC, 2012.

Kennedy, Pat. *How Much Do You Really Know about the Indianapolis 500?* Bloomington, IN: AuthorHouse, 2011.

Kramer, Ralph. *The Indianapolis 500: A Century of Excitement*. Iola, WI: Krause Publishing, 2010.

Websites

To learn more about Inside the Speedway, visit **booklinks.abdopublishing.com.** These links are routinely monitored and updated to provide the most current information available.

INDEX

About the Author

P. K. Daniel is an award-winning editor, reporter, and writer. She spent 15 years at the *San Diego Union-Tribune,* and her work has appeared in *Baseball America,* SBNation.com, TeamUSA.org, *U-T San Diego, The Washington Post, Lower Extremity Review*, and *Sport.*